A Lion Book
an imprint of
Lion Hudson plc
Mayfield House, 256 Banbury Road,
Oxford OX2 7DH, England
www.lionhudson.com
ISBN-13: 978-0-7459-5223-9
ISBN-10: 0-7459-5223-2

First edition 2006
10 9 8 7 6 5 4 3 2 1 0

Typeset in 11.5/14 Calligraph421
Printed and bound in Malaysia

Picture Acknowledgments
pp. 13, 16–17, 32–33, 42–43 and 45 copyright © Getty Images;
pp. 14, 26–27, 28–29 and 30–31 copyright © Punchstock;
pp. 2–3, 5, 6–7, 8–9, 10–11, 18–19, 20–21, 22–23, 24–25, 34–35,
36-37, 38–39, 41 and 46–47 copyright © Jupiterimages.

Text Acknowledgments
pp. 8, 13, 18, 21, 34, 37, 38, 39, 43, 44, 45 Scripture quotations are
taken from the Holy Bible, New International Version, copyright ©
1973, 1978, 1984 International Bible Society. Used by permission
of Zondervan and Hodder and Stoughton Limited. All rights
reserved.

p. 9 Scripture quotation is taken from the Amplified Bible. All
rights reserved. For permission to quote visit www.lockman.org

p. 10 Scripture quotation is taken from the Contemporary English
Version, published by the Bible Societies/Harper Collins Publishers,
copyright © 1991, 1992, 1995 American Bible Society.

pp. 12, 24, 34 Scripture quotations are taken from The Message.
Copyright 1993, 1994, 1995, 1996, 2000, 2001, 2002. Used by
permission of NavPress Publishing Group.

p. 12 poem by Elizabeth B Rooney. Reproduced from *Poems for
Public Worship* by permission of Kevin Mayhew Ltd, Buxhall,
Stowmarket, IP14 3BW, UK. www.kevinmayhewltd.com License
no. 601011.

pp. 16, 17, 30 Scripture quotations are taken from the Living Bible
Edition, copyright © Tyndale House Publishers 1971. All rights
reserved.

p. 17 Scripture quotation is taken from the Revised Standard
Version published by Harper Collins Publishers, copyright © 1989
by the Division of Christian Education of the National Council of
the Churches of Christ in the USA, and is used by permission. All
rights reserved.

pp. 23, 29 Scripture quotations are taken from the New Revised
Standard Version published by Harper Collins Publishers, copyright
© 1989 by the Division of Christian Education of the National
Council of the Churches of Christ in the USA, and are used by
permission. All rights reserved.

pp. 31, 43 Scripture quotations are taken from the Good News
Bible published by The Bible Societies/Harper Collins Publishers,
copyright © 1966, 1971, 1976, 1992 American Bible Society.

THE RESTFUL HEART

Written and compiled
by Liz Babbs

LION

DEDICATED TO MY

FAMILY AND FRIENDS

CONTENTS

INTRODUCTION   8

OVERLOAD   10

LETTING GO   14

CHILLING OUT   18

THE GIFT OF TIME   23

STRESS-LESS   28

CREATED TO ENJOY   34

THE SEASONS   39

NEW BEGINNINGS   42

INTRODUCTION

Come with me
by yourselves to
a quiet place and
get some rest.

Mark 6:31

Life is so busy these days that we seem to be speeding permanently down the fast lane of the motorway dashing from one destination to another, with little time to enjoy the view. But we all need time to reflect – time to take a detour along a country lane, to savour the beautiful scenery, listen to birdsong and enjoy the season's colours and aromas. I wonder when you last had the chance to do this. Many of us yearn for time off, for the opportunity to rediscover life's pauses and quiet times.

Busyness is a seductive habit that can
make us feel important. But busyness is
not synonymous with success, and over-
busyness can quickly lead to burnout, job
loss and relationship breakdown. Our
culture, however, often seems to applaud

people whose diaries are like traffic jams. But being
overbooked may suggest a lack of self-control and wisdom,
and may be a sign of weakness rather than strength. I wonder
if your diary is like a traffic jam.

People today are searching for something other than the
consumer rat race, which seems materially to promise so
much, but deliver so little of real or lasting value. We may be
encouraged to buy now and pay later, but consumerism costs,
and it is easy to become a prisoner of our own possessions. It
is not surprising, then, that downsizing is becoming
increasingly popular, as people search for ways to simplify
their lives.

The Restful Heart is born out of my experience of
burnout, and a longing to encourage others to try a different
route – to rediscover life's natural pauses, and to travel at a
slower speed. There is more to life than productivity, goals
and targets. It seems that you're less likely to appreciate your
destination if you haven't enjoyed the journey. Much of our
life is spent travelling on various different journeys, so you
might as well have some fun along the way!

OVERLOAD

Overload is a sign that we're trying to do too much and are in danger of crashing. The Bible speaks with great authority about the importance of a work-life balance and warns us to be well balanced, because excess in one area of our lives can lead to problems in another. The situation, however, is reversible. Try keeping a journal of your day so that you can see how much activity you are squeezing into 24 hours. Every minute of every day does not need to be filled. And it may not be just you that's over-scheduled, but your whole family! Research shows that regular breaks increase productivity and creativity – so they are an investment of time rather than a waste of it. Try showing your work diary to a friend or partner so that you can be held accountable. They may be able to see ways in which you can cut back on your activities and restore a sense of balance to your life again. Excessive busyness can be addictive, but the law of balance tells us that if we have excess in one area, we'll pay for it in another. So why not act now before it's too late?

VOCATION

It's better
If you take
One day
Or just one minute
At a time

And don't make promises
That you can't keep.
And better,
When you fall,
If you can laugh
As well as weep.

Elizabeth B Rooney

The world of the generous gets larger and larger;
the world of the stingy gets smaller and smaller.

Proverbs 11:24

TREADMILL

Trapped on a treadmill:
activity levels rising,
performance-related pay,
no longer have any say.

I'm in emotional turmoil
running from base to base,
unable to make a decision,
unable to create some space.

Pulled in one direction,
snookered by another.
Caught between living
and meaninglessly
existing.

My eyes are ever on the Lord,
for only he will release my feet from the snare.

Psalm 25:15

FASTER,
FASTER

Fast, faster and faster still
life whizzes by
with no time to chill.

Slow, slower and slower still
can achieve the same objective
and get the task fulfilled.

Blessed are the simple, for they shall have much peace.

Thomas à Kempis

Letting Go

I'm forever trying to de-clutter my house and keep on top of my paperwork so that I can work more efficiently. But there is just as much clutter in my spiritual life too. Worry, anger,

busyness, frustration, self-pity, jealousy and fear can take up a lot of my inner space. All this internal clutter can rob me of the joy of today, if I allow it to. Even my more positive aspirations can become clutter too if they become an obsession in my life.

In order to know what to discard, we need to have an awareness of the things that are cluttering our lives and where our lives might be out of balance. Try asking yourself the following question: If you were told that you had only 48 hours left on earth, how would you spend your time?

It is not our work that defines us, but who we are and how we treat other people.

Time alone

Time to be

Time   to   let
                    g
                       o

No man ever
became great
or good except
through many
and great mistakes.

William E Gladstone

Time to leave behind.

Anxiety is a thin stream of fear trickling
through the mind. If encouraged, it cuts a
channel into which all other thoughts are
drained.

Arthur Somers Roche

In ordinary life we hardly realize that we
receive a great deal more than we give,
and that it is only with gratitude that life
becomes rich.

Dietrich Bonhoeffer

A MOMENT OF JOY

Light shines
on this precious moment
and I am drawn
from the heaviest of
preoccupations
into an expansive vision
arching in rainbow colours
across the skyline
of my imagination.
Myriad possibilities
rain down like stars
and I know that I have tasted joy –
the joy of the moment,
the joy that is today.

Commit your work to the Lord,
and then your plans will succeed.

Proverbs 16:3

To forgive is to set a prisoner free
and discover the prisoner was you.

Source unknown

Do not neglect to show hospitality to strangers, for thereby some have entertained angels unawares.

Hebrews 13:2

If you want to know what God wants you to do – ask him, and he will gladly tell you... But when you ask him, be sure that you really expect him to tell you.

James 1:5–6

ChILLING OUT

My soul finds rest
in God alone.

Psalm 62:1

In our frenetic, demanding and complex
world, our bodies and souls cry out for
rest. But then, we were created to need
rest – it is not only a physical necessity
but also a spiritual law and we ignore
it at our peril. 'Six days you shall
labour and do all your work, but the
seventh day is a Sabbath to the Lord
your God. On it you shall not do any
work...' (Deuteronomy 5:13-14). Even
God rested after he created the world!
Rest is like a savings account that
allows our body time to repair itself. If
we rob this account, our body suffers as
a result. Rest is about relaxing, not
collapsing, so you don't need to worry
that you'll never get going again.

My Presence will go with you,
and I will give you rest.

Exodus 33:14

SERENITY PRAYER

God
grant me
the serenity
to accept the things
I cannot change
courage
to change
the things I can
and the wisdom
to know
the difference.

Reinhold Niebuhr

God is a friend of silence. We cannot find him in noise or agitation. Nature – trees, flowers, grass – grows in silence.

Mother Teresa

The Lord will fight for you; you need only to be still.

Exodus 14:14

Deep peace of the running wave to you,
Deep peace of the flowing air to you,
Deep peace of the quiet earth to you,
Deep peace of the shining stars to you,
Deep peace of the Son of peace to you.

Celtic blessing – source unknown

God can do everything and I can do nothing. But if I offer this nothing in prayer to God, everything becomes possible to me.

Carlo Carretto

Stillness
is
effectively
     a
   thankfulness
for
the
gift
of
life.

Loss Pettersen

Without silence,
words lose their meaning.

The GIfT of TIME

Teach us to count our
days that we may
gain a wise heart.

Psalm 90:12

People seem to be in a rush constantly – earning, possessing, grabbing and achieving. But if we knew that we only had weeks or months to live our attitude to time would inevitably change. Many people who face this reality know only too well how precious life is and how quickly time can run out.

Time is a gift, so we need to use it wisely.

Each week we have 168 hours deposited in our bank account – I wonder how you spend your 168 hours. You might like to assess your use of time by drawing a pie chart – this will help you to highlight the proportion of time you're giving to your job, family, friends, holidays, leisure interests and so on. When you've completed this, try drawing your 'dream' pie chart – which represents how you'd *really* like to spend your time. Now compare the two charts and see where it might be possible to make some life changes to help realize your dreams.

ThE GIFT OF TODAY

Each day is a gift
if you learn how to live in it.
Each moment precious
when you know
it could be
your
last.

Look at the birds, free and unfettered, not tied down
to a job description, careless in the care of God. And
you count far more to him than birds.

Matthew 6:26

Waiting sharpens desire.
In fact it helps us recognize where
our real desires lie.

David Runcorn

TODAY'S PROMISE

Today
is an empty page.
A wonderful space.
An open canvas for me to fill
with a kaleidoscope of colours
and shades of my choosing.
An endless palate of possibilities.

Slow down! Speed cameras can be an annoying nuisance, but at least they remind us to slow down. We all need this reminder as we rush around trying to cram as much as possible into each day. I believe that life was not meant to be lived at such a pace. In our rush we have lost the ability to be patient. We expect everything to be instant and sometimes become angry when we're required to wait. Little wonder, then, that many people now experience office rage as well as road rage! All this pent-up anger fuels our stress levels and has a detrimental effect on our health. So try venting any latent anger by reciting my 'Irritable Vowel Syndrome' poem and then relax and read my little antidote to road rage!

IRRITABLE VOWEL SYNDROME

Agitated
Exasperated
Infuriated
Outraged
Ulcerated

R... now that feels better, doesn't it!

SPEED CAMERAS

I've been clocked;
I've been done,
with a speeding fine to come.
Can you believe it –
they're telling me I've got to pay,
even though I was on foot today?

You see they're bringing in a new law,
one they've never tried before –
speed cameras for people,
to help slow them down.
It's a new government initiative
in cities and in towns.
Said to help beat stress
and take the burden off the NHS.

But now I've got three points of strife
and they say that I could be
disqualified for life!

STRESS-LESS

Many people don't have the art of relaxation and don't know how to switch off from work, so here are some ideas to help you de-stress and chill out:

body

♦ Build in regular rest times. If you neglect yourself, you won't have anything to give to others.

♦ Make sure you exercise; it's a great stress-buster and releases your feel-good endorphins.

♦ Smiling creates fewer wrinkles than frowning. Learn to smile like a child – you'll not only brighten up your day but everyone else's, too!

♦ Take your time. Rushing around multitasking creates stress.

♦ Eat healthily and restrict your caffeine intake.

♦ Listen to your body – it will tell you what it needs.

♦ Drink lots of water. You may be tired because you're dehydrated.

♦ Try having a massage or learn how to self-massage.

♦ Make sure you have at least one day for recreation each week.

♦ To revive your energy, try power napping for 20 minutes each day.

♦ Book holidays into your diary – they are essential and will help you to work more productively.

♦ Try taking a long hot bath with some relaxing oils and just lie back and enjoy...

♦ Don't allow your bank holidays to be hijacked by DIY or other jobs. Have a break away or spend some quality time with family or friends.

♦ Look after your body – it's sacred and is a temple of the Holy Spirit. So treat it with respect. You can't buy another one off the shelf!

MIND

- If you can worry, you can meditate, so try reflecting on positive life-affirming statements rather than your problems. It will help you to unwind and refocus.

- Learn some relaxation techniques. When your body relaxes, your mind will also relax.

- Maintain healthy sleeping patterns. Unplug from your day and make a conscious effort to leave the office behind.

- Treat yourself regularly to something you enjoy.

- Try taking up a new hobby or interest.

- Don't be chained to the office while you're on holiday – ditch the mobile phone and laptop.

- Don't bottle up your problems – chat them through with a close friend instead. A problem shared could well be a problem halved!

- Keep a journal and vent your feelings in there. Research shows that writing can be very therapeutic.

- *Carpe diem* – seize the day. It may be hard to live in the moment, but it's important to keep trying.

- Keep on top of your filing system and de-clutter your house before it becomes another stress factor.

- Do for others what you want them to do for you (Matthew 7:12).

- Find something bigger than yourself to believe in. Research shows that people of faith are happier and healthier.

SPIRIT

◆ Visit a local church or cathedral and enjoy the tranquillity and peace of a sacred place.

◆ Play some relaxing instrumental music (like the CD with this book) and allow it to transport you to another world.

◆ Surround yourself with natural objects, colourful scented flowers and beautiful imagery to brighten up your day.

◆ Go for a long countryside walk or visit some beautiful gardens.

◆ Set aside a special room or comfortable chair dedicated to relaxation and meditation.

◆ Laughter is great medicine, so book in regular sessions. Put on your favourite comedy video or DVD or spend time with friends who make you laugh. Being cheerful keeps you healthy (Proverbs 17:22).

◆ Try going on a retreat – it's like taking a special holiday with God.

◆ Don't become a style slave, trying to keep up with the latest fashions and consumer trends – identify your spiritual needs and elevate these above your material needs.

The Relaxation Zone

Did you know that relaxation improves your reaction to stress and depression and can decrease your chances of developing certain health problems, such as heart disease and cancer?

Try these simple relaxation techniques:

Breathing Exercise

- Sitting with your back well supported and with both your feet on the floor, close your eyes and become aware of your breathing.

- Now allow your breathing to become deeper and slower.

- Try breathing in for two counts, holding your breath for two counts and then breathing out for four counts. Repeat several times.

- Now try breathing in for three counts, holding your breath for three counts and breathing out for six counts. Repeat several times.

DIY Massage

Gently rub your shoulders and become aware of any tension spots and then massage them firmly. Now, using both hands, firmly massage the whole of your scalp as though you were shampooing your hair. Ah... now that feels better, doesn't it?

MEDITATION

1 Begin by sitting or lying down in a comfortable position, where you won't be disturbed.

2 Imagine that you can see a large pile of papers on your desk, or a long list of emails cluttering the inbox of your computer. These papers and emails represent the pressure of all the things you've got to do.

3 Now imagine yourself putting these papers into a drawer, or your emails into a special folder labelled 'to action later'.

4 Now relax, close your eyes and become aware of your breathing getting deeper and slower. Visualize a favourite place you like to visit – it might be a beach or countryside walk, a local park, church or garden. Allow your mind to travel to that place now, so that you can picture yourself there.

5 Savour the beauty and tranquillity of this place for several minutes, enjoying the scenery, sounds, colours and aromas. Now slowly repeat the following affirmation to yourself:

> *In the storms of life,*
> *I am still.*
> *In the noise of life,*
> *I find silence.*
> *In the busyness of life,*
> *I remain at peace.*

6 Finally, see the words RELAX... PEACE... BE STILL drifting across the screen saver of your mind. Remember these key words as you open your eyes and begin to move on with the rest of your day.

CREATED TO ENJOY

Creation is a window through which we see God.

The Bible tells us that all things were made by and for Christ (Colossians 1:16), so one of the ways we can worship God is by caring for creation. God created the earth for our enjoyment. But he also called us to be responsible for the earth by being good stewards of it. In Genesis, Adam is sent into the garden to *till and keep* the land, which in the original Hebrew language means to 'serve' and 'preserve' it.

For every animal of the forest is mine,
and the cattle on a thousand hills.
I know every bird in the mountains,
and the creatures of the field are mine.

Psalm 50:10–11

Walk into the fields and look at the wildflowers... have you ever seen colour and design quite like it?

Luke 12:27

SANCTUARY

Through creation
I am restored
renewed
and healed.

SEASCAPE

I love
the sea.
I love basking
in her presence
feeling the surge
of her spray upon my lips and
allowing her energy to touch my soul.

SUNBATHING

Nothing trumpets
outrageous beauty
like the sunflower.
Nature's green
and yellow satellite dish
cranes her neck
towards the sun
faithfully tracking every movement.
Sunbathing in its glory
she beams a contented smile
upon all creation.

Skyline   SUNRISE
streaked with
orange and saffron
herald the sun's majestic
rise, as it peeps its head
above the horizon
and gold plates
everything
with its
radiance.

He who forms the mountains,
creates the wind,
and reveals his thoughts to man,
he who turns dawn to darkness,
and treads the high places of the earth –
the Lord God Almighty is his name

Amos 4:13

In his hand is the life of every creature
and the breath of all mankind.

Job 12:10

In him we live and move and have our being.

Acts 17:28

The fool says in his heart,
'There is no God.'

Psalm 14:1

the seasons

See! The winter
is past; the rains
are over
and gone.

Song of Songs 2:11

As we journey, we discover that some things only last for a season.

The spiritual life is often compared to the seasons, each with its own unique opportunities and challenges. In our fast-lived culture where people can work all hours round the clock, it's easy to forget the natural sense of rhythm and pattern that we are created to enjoy: 'There was evening, and there was morning – the first day' (Genesis 1:5). Daily and seasonal rhythms help us to pace our lives and to experience God. The beauty of the different seasons is also an important reminder of the natural rhythm of life. The Bible tells us that 'to everything there is a season, and a time for every purpose under heaven' (Ecclesiastes 3:1). Every season is special in some way and so is every season of our life, even if it feels more like winter than spring!

For as the rain and the snow come down from heaven,
and do not return there until they have watered the earth,
making it bring forth and sprout,
giving seed to the sower and bread to the eater,
so shall my word...
not return to me empty.

Isaiah 55:10–11

SPRING HOPE

In the spring valley,
tiny snowdrops
push their proud heads through
ice-frozen ground
and shafts of light
beam sunshine moments
on love's tender shoots.

SUMMERTIME

lazy hazy days
of carefree
a b a n d o n m e n t

SUNDANCE

The sun
awakens
the palate of an artist,
sharpens
the pen of a writer,
and dances
upon the waters
of our imagination.

The
autumn
sun rises
slowly into the sky,
radiating a kaleidoscope
of colour, while autumn leaves
dance across roof tops and
hover through the air,
painting pathways of
gold.

NEW BEGINNINGS

Heaven touches earth as we seek to touch heaven.

Andy Raine

Running a race is a wonderful metaphor for our journey through life. But our race is more like a marathon than a sprint, so we need to pace ourselves carefully. However, there is little point in running if we don't have a reason to run or the finishing line isn't even in sight. The beginning of a new year is a time when people make resolutions. I wonder if you can remember yours. But you don't need to wait until the new year to make changes to your life – why not begin now by listing the top ten things you'd most like to change?

NEW BEGINNINGS

New year,
new hope,
fresh challenges.
A chance to let go
– to leave behind
what was,
and adventure
into what will be...

Do not store up riches for yourselves here on earth... Instead, store up riches for yourselves in heaven... For your heart will always be where your riches are.

Matthew 6:19–21

Dance as though no one is watching you.
Love as though you've never been hurt.
Sing as though no one can hear you.
Live as though heaven is on earth.

Source unknown

'No eye has seen, no ear has heard, no mind has conceived what God has prepared for those who love him.'

1 Corinthians 2:9

Fear knocked at the door. Faith opened it and there was no one there.

Source unknown

FAITH IS... Faith is silence filled with expectation.
Prayer pregnant with hope.
Trust in deepest darkness.
A light shining the way.

Faith is waiting and knowing,
allowing God to direct.
Faith is listening and growing
as he carefully orders each step.

A man who prays is a man standing with his hands open to the world.

Henri Nouwen

'For I know the plans I have for you... plans to prosper you and not to harm you, plans to give you hope and a future.'

Jeremiah 29:11

Let us make God the beginning and end of our love, for he is the fountain from which all good things flow.

Richard Rolle

But those who hope in the Lord will renew their strength.
They will soar on wings like eagles;
they will run and not grow weary,
they will walk and not be faint.

Isaiah 40:31

You can contact
the author on
liz@lizbabbs.com
or via her website
www.lizbabbs.com

track titles

OVERLOAD

LETTING GO

CHILLING OUT

THE GIFT OF TIME

STRESS-LESS

CREATED TO ENJOY

THE SEASONS

NEW BEGINNINGS